7

AUTHOR'S NOTE

Mickey Charles Mantle—named after baseball Hall of Famer Gordon "Mickey" Cochrane—was born on October 20, 1931, in Spavinaw, Oklahoma. When he was four, his family moved to the town of Commerce. To say Mantle had a rough childhood is putting it mildly—aside from poverty, he endured abuse by an adult and older children that no doubt scarred him for life. This book celebrates the good and amazing things he was still able to do, and the joy he brought his fans.

Though Mickey had some bad breaks, he was lucky to have spent his entire Major League career with the New York Yankees. During the 1950s, New York was the capital of baseball, with its three great teams: the Yankees, the Giants, and the Brooklyn Dodgers, all of whom were usually in the playoffs, and often in the World Series. Of course, the Yankees were the best, winning five World Series in a row (and seven altogether) under the management of Casey Stengel. Mickey Mantle was Stengel's prize player. Believing him to be potentially the greatest ever, he took Mickey under his wing. But the Commerce Comet, as Mickey was immediately nicknamed upon joining the Yankees, did not live up to Stengel's expectations—perhaps no one could have.

Still, Mantle is generally regarded as one of the greatest sluggers, and THE greatest switch-hitter, in history—and holds some switch-hitting records to this day: single-season home runs (54 in 1961), career on-base percentage (.421), and career slugging average (.557). Mantle boasts many impressive numbers in addition to the stats listed in this book: the second-most games played in New York Yankees history (2,401), the seventeenth-most career home runs in major league history (536), and the eighth-most walks in major league history (1,733). On May 22, 1963, he came closer than any other Major League player to hitting a ball out of Yankee Stadium—it hit the 110-foot-high façade.

Off the field, Mickey Mantle is most famous for having suffered from the disease of alcoholism. He died on August 13, 1995—of liver cancer caused by the alcoholism. Less than two years earlier, Mantle had undergone treatment and stopped drinking. He had publicly apologized for his behavior, encouraging other alcoholics to seek treatment. All I can say about Mickey Mantle's off-field behavior is that I once met him in a Howard Johnson's when I was a child, and he was very friendly to me. I was a fan.

FOR MY FATHER -J.W.

FOR MY SONS, TREVOR, WHO GOT TO MEET THE MICK, AND EVAN, WHO LOVES THE GAME AS MUCH AS HIS DAD DOES -C.F.P.

 Published in the United States by Schwartz & Wade Books, an imprint of Random House Children's Books, a division of Penguin Random House LLC, New York. • Schwartz & Wade Books and the colophon are trademarks of Penguin Random House LLC. • Library of Congress Cataloging-in-Publication Data is available upon request. ISBN 978-1-101-93352-7 (hc)—ISBN 978-1-101-93353-4 (lib. bdg.)—ISBN 978-1-101-93354-1 (ebook) • The illustrations in this book were rendered in acrylics and pencil.

MANUFACTURED IN CHINA • 2 4 6 8 10 9 7 5 3 1 • First Edition

written by **JONAH WINTER** & illustrated by **C. F. PAYNE**

schwartz & wade books • new york

Mickey Mantle: He had the perfect baseball player name. Mickey—boyish, all-American, it rolls right off the tongue. MANTLE—carved stone. RAW STRENGTH.

Where Mickey came from, you had to be strong—tough, too: Commerce, Oklahoma. Mining country. A tiny shack, with ten people, three beds, and no indoor plumbing.

His daddy worked in the pitch-black depths of a mine, breathing toxic dust, dodging falling slabs of rock the length of city blocks. It was a hard life—and he wanted better for his son. So he just hauled off and *decided* that Mickey was going to be what he himself had wanted to be: a baseball player.

Mickey, in diapers, had little to say on the topic. He just caught the balls his daddy rolled across the floor . . . and rolled ’em right back.

Mickey never had a choice. Every day, after school, his daddy and his grandpa would stand him up against the shed and throw him tennis balls, teaching him how to hit left- and right-handed, how to be a “switch-hitter.” And Mickey learned—oh, did he learn.

And that kid was *fast*. As legend has it, he learned how to run like the wind while darting to the outhouse, armed with a bat, pursued by the fearsome family rooster. You can look it up!

But here's the head-scratching part: Little Mickey showed few signs of becoming any superstar athlete. He was small for his age. He wet the bed. He had a bone disease that almost caused him to lose a leg. When he was fourteen, his mother had to convince the surgeon not to amputate.

For more than a year, Mickey was in and out of hospitals, getting pumped full of penicillin. But after he recovered, so the story goes . . .

he shot up like Jack's beanstalk. His baseball coach got him a part-time job digging graves and hauling tombstones to bulk him up. By junior year, *the kid was unrecognizable*—bulging muscles, legs like tree trunks. Girls wanted to date him. Boys wanted to BE him. What did Mickey want? Ah, nothin' much—just to be the greatest ballplayer who ever lived. (AND, as he told a friend, to replace the most popular player in the world, the New York Yankees center fielder: *Joltin' Joe DiMaggio.*)

And so it came to pass, one fateful summer night: Mickey's playing for a semipro team, the Baxter Springs Whiz Kids, and who should be driving down the road but a guy named Tom Greenwade—a New York Yankees talent scout. He notices the ballpark lights, pulls over, *and proceeds to witness the best raw baseball talent he has ever seen.*

He walks up to Mickey and asks him how old he is.

"Sixteen," Mickey tells him.

Too young for the major leagues.

Still, he asks, "Would you ever be interested in playing ball for the Yankees?"

Well, you can bet that gave Mickey something to think about!

One year later, on graduation day, he skips the ceremony to go play ball. Greenwade, who'd gotten wind of Mickey's graduation, is back—with dollar signs where his eyes should be. Kid slams TWO home runs—one left-handed, one right-handed. **Cha-ching!** A few days later, Mickey had himself a contract—to play with the Yankees' farm team in Missouri. That was 1949. The world had not yet heard of this greenhorn. But in those two minor league years, the Mickey Mantle legend began.

He could run from home plate to first on a bunt in 2.9 seconds, the fastest in history!

He could round the bases in thirteen seconds flat: so fast he sounded like a team of wild horses. Fast as a cheetah. Faster than a speeding bullet. Fast.

Before spring training begins for the '51 season, the Yanks decide to let him show his stuff—in their big-league lineup. It's March 26: an exhibition game with a California college team. The news guys have already dubbed this shy country boy "the Commerce Comet." Mantle knows that all eyes are on him. He's on deck, his hat pulled down low. He ain't smilin'.

First time up, the Okie gets a pitch that's almost in the dirt—nothing most guys would swing at. Only, Mantle swings. But he doesn't just swing—he CLOBBERS the living tar out of that ball . . .

sends it sailing high above the center field wall . . . toward the practice field for a football team . . . where it lands, right in the middle of a huddle! From there, it apparently bounces off into the sunset. Theories erupted as to how far the ball had traveled. "Five hundred fifty-one feet!" "Six hundred sixty feet!" No one had ever seen anything quite like it. THIS was a new kind of ballplayer.

Oh, if only, *if only,* Mickey could have stayed the way he was on that day, forever young, forever healthy, forever limitless in what he could do. But that is not the Mickey Mantle story. Here's what happened: Mickey's boyhood dream came true—at age nineteen, the Yanks brought him up to the majors, where *he'd replace the aging DiMaggio* in center field when Joe retired at the end of that year. They even posed for photos together—the old star and the young star with the bashful, country-boy smile. *The torch was being passed.* [GULP.] *Greatness would be expected.*

But he did not go home. He went back to the ballpark, and hit by hit by hit, in less than a couple of months, he worked his way back to Yankee Stadium *just in time for the moment that would change his life:*

October 5, 1951. World Series, Game Two. Yanks vs. New York Giants. Fifth inning—Giants are up. Who should be standing in the batter's box but Mickey's soon-to-be archrival, the great Willie Mays. Count is 2 and 2. Yankees pitcher Eddie Lopat gives Mays something he can hit, and Mays knocks a pop fly to right-center field—smack-dab between DiMaggio and Mantle. Mantle gives chase, barreling a zillion miles an hour. Meanwhile, DiMaggio is also closing in on the ball. At the very last second, Joe D shouts, "I got it!" and Mantle slams on the brakes—right where a drainage pipe is sticking up out of the ground. His right foot catches on it. Mantle goes down, his face wrenched in pain. The crowd goes silent. And Mantle just lies there, motionless. He looks like he's dead.

EXIT
EXIT

Turns out Mickey's right knee has basically become detached from his ligaments. He's carried off on a stretcher. After this, he would never be as fast, and he would always be in pain.

A few months later, his father dies of cancer. The most important man in twenty-year-old Mickey Mantle's universe is gone.

If you think this story's over, then you know nothing about Mickey Mantle. Okay, so he'd never get from home plate to first base in 2.9 seconds again. After the injury, it takes him *3.1 seconds*—still an unofficial record.

And "the Mick," as he was called, seemed to get even bigger. His arms and shoulders were the envy of the baseball world. But plenty of guys have muscles. What Mantle had was EMOTION, a FIRE inside that caused him to CRUSH the ball, like on April 17, 1953, in Griffith Stadium in Washington, DC, where he sent one ball not just outside the park, but *so far* outside . . . that it landed in someone's backyard blocks away! The best anyone can tell, it traveled roughly 540 feet—which, if that's true, is by far the longest measured homer in major league history, and the first "tape-measure home run."

NY

Every at-bat, his cap pulled down low, it was like he was daring pitchers to throw a strike. And mostly, pitchers didn't dare. Five seasons, he held the record for walks.

And he was the greatest switch-hitter in history. Put a lefty up against him—he hits a right-handed homer. Put a righty up, he parks one left-handed. As Cleveland's Bob Feller said, "Mantle had no weak spots." And Feller would've known—he once gave up a home run to the Mick that left the stadium. "What'd you throw him?" the Hall of Famer was asked. "A baseball," he answered.

What Mickey was able to do was nearly a miracle, considering. Before every game, he had to wrap his right leg in bandages to keep his knee from popping out. And there were many, *many* more injuries—broken bones, pulled muscles, strains, sprains—from his shoulders to his feet.

After games, he would just lie on his sofa and moan. Why was he injured so much? Because when you play that hard—with a body that's already damaged goods—you're bound to get hurt, *repeatedly.*

But, despite this, Mickey was a big reason the Yanks went to the World Series twelve times—and to this day he holds the records for most home runs, RBIs, extra base hits, runs, walks, and total bases in World Series history. And though he played with a bum knee, in 1956 he led the league in batting average, home runs, and RBIs, winning the Triple Crown—something never done by Babe Ruth, Joe DiMaggio, Willie Mays, or Hank Aaron. Mantle did it, though every swing of the bat caused excruciating pain.

NEW YORK

Just trotting around the bases after a home run was painful—you could tell by his limp. Once, in Baltimore, it looked like he could barely make it. By the time he crossed home plate, there were tears streaming down his face—but it turned out this wasn't because of his legs. It was because of the cheering fans, all on their feet. You see, Mickey was one of the most beloved players in baseball history—which shocked him. The way he figured it, he hadn't been as good as he *could have been.* He hadn't lived up to everyone's great expectations. He hadn't been *perfect.*

The way the fans figured it, though, none of that mattered. They knew Mickey wasn't perfect. But they also knew that to watch a guy do what he did, with that body, could take your breath away.

7